VISITOR PASS

Planning a trip to the Moon? Here's all you need to know about our nearest neighbour in space. Follow us on a journey of discovery!

For Elliot, who loves looking up – B.L.
For Annie – P.C.

First published 2025 by Walker Books Ltd
87 Vauxhall Walk, London SE11 5HJ

2 4 6 8 10 9 7 5 3 1

EU Authorized Representative: HackettFlynn Ltd, 36 Cloch Choirneal, Balrothery, Co. Dublin, K32 C942, Ireland. EU@walkerpublishinggroup.com

This book has been typeset in Amasis and Nevis

Printed in China

British Library Cataloguing in Publication Data: a catalogue record for this book is available from the British Library

ISBN 978-1-5295-1730-9

www.walker.co.uk

THE MOON
A Visitor's Guide

BEN LERWILL

Illustrated by PATRICK CORRIGAN

WALKER BOOKS
AND SUBSIDIARIES
LONDON • BOSTON • SYDNEY • AUCKLAND

What's this, floating high in the starry sky?

It is silent, and beautiful, and ancient.

It shines like silver in the quiet of the night.

We call it
THE MOON.

THE MOON
384,400 KM

When we look at the Moon, we're staring across **hundreds of thousands** of miles of space. The Moon is 238,900 miles, or 384,400 kilometres away from Earth. That's more than a million Eiffel Towers stood one on top of the other –

OR 75 MILLION GIRAFFES!

It takes three whole days to fly there in a spaceship. If we could walk there, it would take nine years – without stopping!

The Moon is always on the move. It takes around a **month** for it to circle Earth once. As it travels through space, the side of the Moon facing the Sun gets covered in sunlight. Over 30 days, our view of the Moon goes from being completely **dark** to completely **bright** – then back again!

NEW MOON

This is when we can't see any light on the Moon at all because the sunlit part is turned away from us.

HALF-MOON

This is when half of the Moon is in darkness and the other half in sunlight.

FULL MOON
In the middle of every 30-day cycle, we can see the whole Moon glowing like a giant ball.
LUNAR ECLIPSE
Once or twice a year, the Moon passes right through Earth's shadow. Direct sunlight can't reach its surface, so the Moon's glow becomes dimmer.
But here's an interesting question:
HAS THE MOON ALWAYS BEEN THERE?

And here's an interesting answer:
NO, IT HASN'T!
To find out more, we need to travel WAY back in time.
Scientists think Earth was formed about 4.5 billion years ago.
At first, it had no Moon.
Then one day, something big happened.
Something very big.

An object the size of Mars,
hurtling at top speed across the galaxy, smashed straight into Earth.
Experts believe the collision sent HUGE chunks of rock flying into space,
which eventually clumped together and became the Moon.
So although the Moon
is very, very old, it's not
QUITE as old as the world!

We aren't the only planet with a moon.

In total, our solar system has nearly 300 moons. Only the Jupiter moons of Ganymede, Callisto and Io and the Saturn moon of Titan are larger than ours.

So how big is our Moon?

Its circumference – or the distance all the way around its middle – is 6,783 miles, or 10,917 kilometres. That makes it four times smaller than Earth.

When we see a full moon in the sky, its diameter – or the distance from left to right – is 2,160 miles, or 3,475 kilometres. That's roughly the same as the width of Australia.

Like Earth, the Moon is made of **rock**. But there's a big difference. On Earth, a layer of gases, known as the atmosphere, blocks some of the Sun's rays and traps heat at night. But the Moon has **almost no atmosphere**. This means it gets **VERY hot** in the day and **VERY cold** at night.

In full sunlight, the temperature on the Moon can reach 127°C. That's double the hottest temperature ever recorded in the Sahara Desert!

But in darkness, the temperature on the Moon can fall to minus 173°C. That's double the coldest temperature ever recorded in Antarctica!

Nothing lives here. The Moon has only small amounts of water and ice, but its surface is covered in what scientists call "seas".

The biggest sea is called the Ocean of Storms – but it's not an ocean, and the Moon doesn't have storms!

Well, these seas are actually **big craters**. Most of these craters were formed by meteorites crashing into the surface, hundreds of millions of years ago.

Back then, the Moon also had **active volcanoes**. When lava oozed out of the volcanoes, it flowed into the craters and hardened.

The Moon is **VERY** important to us. To understand why, we have to understand **gravity**.

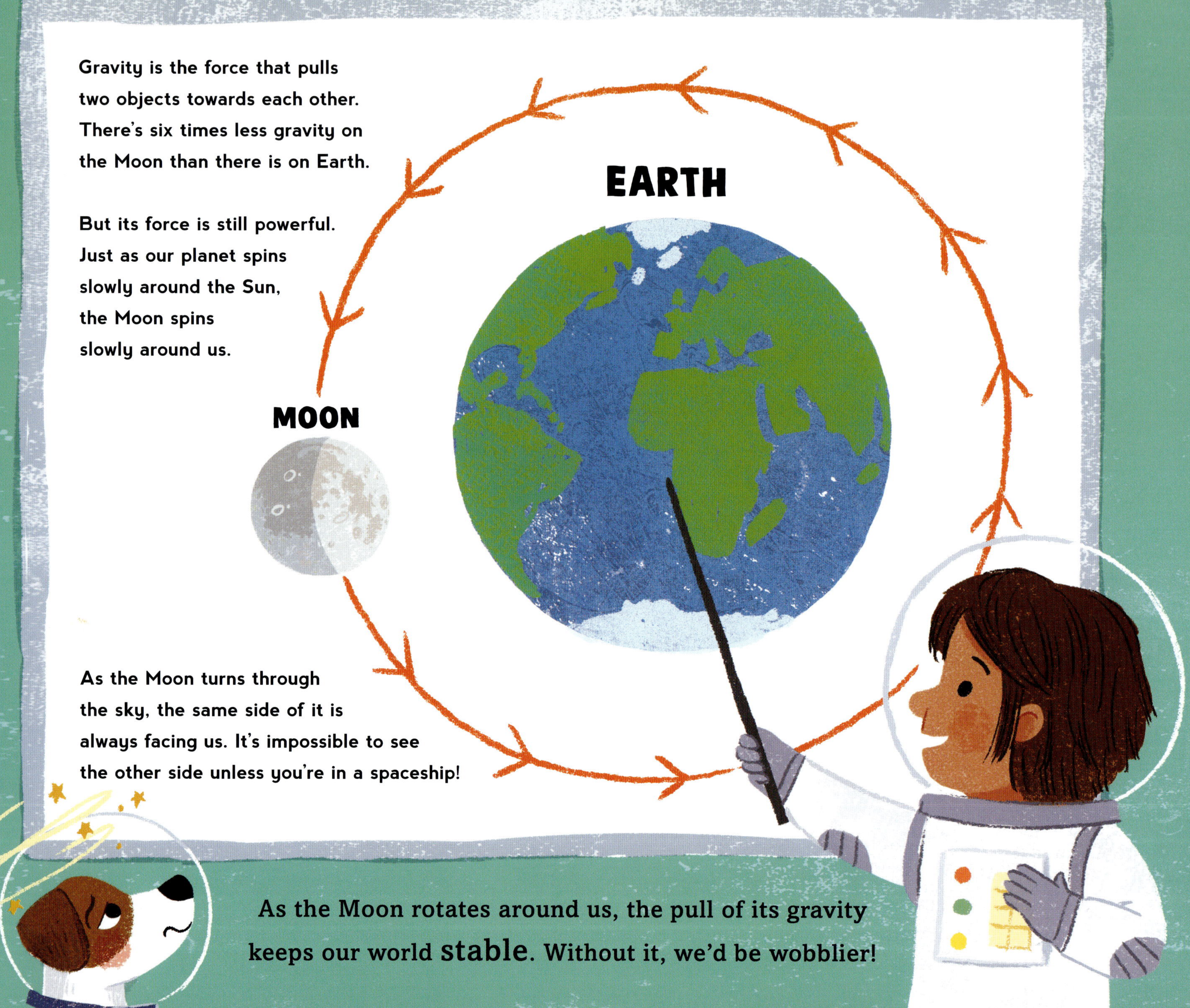

Gravity is the force that pulls two objects towards each other. There's six times less gravity on the Moon than there is on Earth.

But its force is still powerful. Just as our planet spins slowly around the Sun, the Moon spins slowly around us.

As the Moon turns through the sky, the same side of it is always facing us. It's impossible to see the other side unless you're in a spaceship!

As the Moon rotates around us, the pull of its gravity keeps our world **stable**. Without it, we'd be wobblier!

The Moon's gravity also has a big effect on our **oceans**.

When the sea's **tide** rises or falls, it's because water is being drawn, ever so gently, towards the Moon.

Our Moon has been high above us for billions of years. But in **July 1969**, something very special happened.

A spaceship carrying **three astronauts** blasted off from Earth.

The astronauts' footprints are still there today!

Two of the astronauts on board became the first people ever to walk on the surface of the Moon.

Their names were **Neil Armstrong** and **Buzz Aldrin**. The spaceship's name was **Apollo 11**.

Between 1969 and 1972, five more spaceships took astronauts to the Moon, to carry out experiments and learn more about space travel. But sending astronauts to the Moon was expensive.

Since then, other spacecraft have sent **robots** to the surface, but none have sent people.

For more than 50 years, **not one** astronaut landed on the Moon.

The Yutu-2 lunar rover was the first robot to explore the far side of the Moon. It landed in 2019 – and it's still up there now. It's only slightly bigger than a supermarket trolley.

But the world is making BIG plans.

Plans for astronauts to return with more dreams of discovery.

We all live under the **same** Moon.

Dinosaurs saw it in the sky. So did the **ancient Egyptians**, the **Romans** and the **Vikings**. The Moon has looked down on **every human** who has ever walked the Earth.

And best of all?

One day, **YOU** could be the next astronaut up there.

THE HISTORY OF

2 JANUARY 1959

The Soviet Union – a giant country made up of Russia and some of its neighbours – launches an uncrewed spacecraft, Luna 1. It flies past the Moon.

3 MARCH 1959

The USA launches its own uncrewed spacecraft, Pioneer 4. Like Luna 1, it travels past the Moon.

14 SEPTEMBER 1959

The uncrewed Soviet spacecraft Luna 2 bumps down onto the Moon, becoming the first human-made object on its surface.

24 DECEMBER 1968

The crew of American spacecraft Apollo 8 become the first people to see it up close. Their flight makes ten circuits around the Moon.

DID YOU

The list of items left on the Moon from previous missions includes golf balls, flags, a Christian Bible, moon buggies, a family photo – and almost 100 bags of astronaut poo!

The Moon gets slightly further away from us every year – but only by about 4 centimetres. That's less than the little finger of an astronaut glove.

MOON EXPLORATION

20 JULY 1969

Apollo 11 astronauts Neil Armstrong and Buzz Aldrin become the first humans to land and walk on the Moon.

11 DECEMBER 1972

The astronauts of Apollo 17 become the sixth American crew to land on the Moon. No humans will return for well over 50 years.

TODAY

Space agencies worldwide continue their Moon explorations. Russia, the USA, China, India and Japan have all now landed uncrewed spacecraft here.

THE FUTURE

It's only a matter of time before humans walk on the Moon again. But who will be the lucky astronauts – and when will they get there?

KNOW?

This is the side of the Moon that faces us.

OCEAN OF STORMS

SEA OF SERENITY

SEA OF TRANQUILITY

APOLLO 15

APOLLO 17

APOLLO 11

APOLLO 12

APOLLO 14

APOLLO 16

The map shows where astronauts have landed!

Because the Moon circles us, we call it a natural satellite. It's the only natural satellite we have. Earth has THOUSANDS of other satellites, but they're all made by humans.